Rick: "So this is where you work, Turtle?"

Turtle: "Only when da surf's bad.
Cause' when da surf's good,
nobody works!"

— (FROM THE FILM, NORTH SHORE)

Homer Simpson: "Marge, the
dog doesn't count as a kid."

Cover Design: Eric Maki

Front Cover Photo: John Bilderback (www.surfphotos.com)

Photo & Art Credits: Kim Peterson, Heather L. Erickson, Bruce Hooker, Edward J. Hepp III, Universal Pictures, Disney, Wavefest, Waxfoot Surf Sho Desert Rose Productions, Steve Castellotti, Elizabeth Spurr, Tahiti Tourism Amazing Animals NZ, Roxy, A.K. Crump, Ruff Wear, Billabong, Billabong Odyssey, Surfing Australia, Sunde White, the Landrum Family, VonZipper, Gordon and Smith, Liquid Shredder, National Geographic Channel, Cinefl Productions, Quiksilver, Tim Riedel, EG Fratantaro, Sony Picture Classics

Written contributions by: Bruce Hooker, Edward J. Hepp III, Brian Musial Michael Congdon and Annie, Steve Castellotti, Elizabeth Spurr, Carolyn Press Mckenzie, Lyn Richards, Steve Pike, Sunde White, A.K. Crump, Lorai Poersch

Many thanks are due to Bruce Jenkins, Heather L. Erickson, Buddy, Mugs, Part-Ex, Rob from Critters of the Cinema, Bailey, Skateboard Mike, Haggi Scott Bass, American Humane Association, Dee, Matt Meyerson, Toby, Chc per, Luke Millen, Michael W. Spence, John-Paul Eatock, Bob Strickland, Sai Cruz Surf Museum, Aqua Surf Shop, Wavescape.co.za, Jason Carrougher, Kim Peterson, Randy Green, Heather McDonald, David Madden, Dunny McDonough, Al Partenan

## tcb cafe publishing

PO Box 471706
San Francisco, CA 94147

# The Dog's Guide to

# Surfing

# Table of Contents

*Sini,*
*Beach lover and Surf Dog companion*
*of Kim Peterson*

# What is a Surf Dog?

Surf Dogs are everywhere. On beach blankets and car logos, on rock bands and kids' pajamas, the name of the "surf dog" has been part of North American, South African, Hawaiian, New Zealand and Australian cultures for at least a half century. The image of the "surf dog," or as some people write it, "surf dogz," conjures up feelings of being outdoors, on the beach near a bonfire with friends, dancing around watching the tide, waiting for the next chance to jump on a board. If someone says that they are a "surf dog," it means they are committed to the surfing life. If someone says that they have a surf dog, it means that dog is committed to them.

Any hound can be a surf dog, regardless of size. Whether they are a Beagle, a Basset or a Saint Bernard, what matters is not their ability, but their desire for companionship and adventure. They have the spirit and willingness to go where no dog has gone before, and are cool with that, as long as they are with their human friends. Walking on the beach, playing in the waves, chasing a Frisbee or having a sandy picnic, any of these show the soul of a true surf dog.

If they are lucky, they may get on a board and hop a curl, and when they land, they will be forever changed. That dog will have dug deep, been high, and reached a new plateau.

As sports journalist and surfer Bruce Jenkins explains, "A few years ago I did a long SURFER magazine piece on Rell Sunn, the late, great Hawaiian surfer. She had a dog named Shane, and Shane surfed with her.

The dog understood where to stand, how to ride out a wave, not to panic when they wiped out. Back on land, the dog was as cool as could be, like he was onto something the other dogs couldn't understand.

Brian Keaulana, the great Makaha surfer and a neighbor of Rell's, told me, 'Once they've been surfing, dogs know they aren't like all the other dogs. They've got a little attitude. They know they're part of something very special.'"

Truer words have never been spoken. But the real truth is that any dog who goes with you to the beach, just to be with you and play, is officially a surf dog.

# Spotting a True Surf Dog

*Stoked Surf Dog,*
*from Mike 'n Heather's Rockabilly Photo Album*

When people are asked if they have ever seen a dog surf, they often will look at you as if it is an incredible question. But inevitably someone steps up with an equally incredible response.

Even if you don't have your own dog to surf with, the memory of witnessing a surf dog on the waves stays with you a very long time. "I'll never forget my first encounters with a surf dog," says former Ocean Beach resident, Heather L. Erickson.

"It was 10 years ago. There was a guy who would take his dog out surfing in front of our house all the time.  He had a separate board for his dog.

The dog would ride out on top of the board with help from his owner, then surf the waves in. The dog would bring his board in his mouth to shore and bark until his owner rode in a wave and took him out again.

It was so cute and funny how his dog would look so relaxed and confident riding the waves, then get so excited, barking to go out  again."

*Above and Right: Surf Dogs in their natural habitat*

# Teach a Dog to Surf with TRUST

So you want to teach your dog how to surf, but don't know where to start? The best way to get off on the right foot is to think about "trust."

Dogs have a much better sense of smell than sight. When they're on dry land they are masters of their domain, and there are a lot of ways for

them to get around on their own. This is the case even if they can't see where they are going as well as a human. The dog's sense of smell is a powerful tool for navigation and identification, and dog's love new and different aromas.

Part of the reason why dogs love to go to the beach is exactly because it is such a crazy area filled with all kinds of cool new odors: fish, kelp, sand, salt, lotion, shells, and even blankets. But what does a dog smell when it's out in the water on a surfboard?

Water.

Where is that smell going to lead him?

Not far.

This is where the dog's trust in you comes in. A dog on a surfboard is a lot more helpless than a dog on shore, and you are the person it relies on to lead the way. Everyone who has had to teach a dog a new trick says that it's always been possible because the dog had trust in them. The same can be said about surfing.

So when you apply the tips, hints, lessons and steps discussed in the THE DOG'S GUIDE TO SURFING, remember that the real reason why they work is not because you are a genius or a natural animal trainer. They work because your dog thinks that you are trustworthy.

Good luck, and have fun!

*Bruce and Buddy, riding tandem*

# Tails from the Nose:
# Buddy the Surf Dog

Our dog Buddy is a soul surfer. Buddy is four years old, an only pup of a litter of ranch dogs. His mother, Nipsy, got into some rat poisoning during her pregnancy, and only one pup survived - Buddy. Buddy was born on a ranch in the foothills of Ventura, California. The ranch has anywhere from 10-20 dogs at a time, 8 of which are Jack Russell Terriers; the rest Border Collies and Corgis. We brought Buddy home when he was just 5 weeks old, along with Nipsy, to stay with us for 2 weeks. After that Buddy stayed with us, and Nipsy returned to the ranch. We also have a 12-year old, Australian Shepard, named Teton, who was born deaf and is Buddy's best friend. Buddy helps Teton and enables him as if he really understands this handicap.

Buddy started his athletic career as a runner, running from 6 to 16 miles per day with my wife Leslie on her daily jogs. Leslie lost her previous running mate Toby, also a Jack Russell Terrier, when he was struck by a car 6 months earlier. Buddy started running when he was about 6 months old, and really took to it. After a couple years of 70 miles per week, Buddy became very strong, with great jumping ability. We also have two children, Megan and Matthew.

Megan takes credit for starting Buddy's surfing career, although I feel that I have brought out his true surfing talent by taking him for 'go outs' so often. Buddy started surfing when he was two years old in Santa Barbara. One day Megan was boogie boarding in the surf, and Buddy was watching. He was barking, running, and apparently waiting for his opportunity to jump on the board. When the board floated into shore without Megan on it, Buddy seized the moment, and hopped right on it. He balanced on the board as it floated in the shallow water like a skim board, barking all the time from the excitement. Megan pulled the board by its leash with Buddy standing on it, and he balanced and barked. He seemed to really be excited and enjoying the ride. Megan then took Buddy into the small surf while he was standing on top of the board, and they caught a little wave in the shore break. Together they rode the wave in, with Buddy on the front of the board and her holding onto the back. Buddy was so excited, barking, jumping off and on the board - he wanted to do it again and again. We each took turns with Buddy, and he just loved it, along with everyone else on the beach who was watching. Because I'm an experienced board and body surfer, I wanted to see how far we could take Buddy with this affinity for surfing.

**PROFILE**

I took Buddy out a little farther each time we surfed, and started letting go of the back of the board after we had ridden the wave for a distance. Each time I would let the board go with Buddy on it sooner and sooner, and let him ride the wave by himself. Buddy learned through trial and error, and several wipeouts, that he needed to adjust to the board and the wave so he wouldn't pearl or wipeout. With time, he learned to move back and lay low for takeoffs, then, after he rode the wave a distance, he could stand up and move forward on the board. Buddy still rides his original Morey Boogie, a 20 year old board, although he has chewed off about 30% of the board, which is affecting it's performance. Buddy is looking for a board sponsor.

During the second summer Buddy really began to get the hang of surfing, and we loved taking him out. Buddy picked up where he left off the previous summer, riding wave after wave, only wiping out about 20% of the time. I learned that he did much better on mushy takeoffs rather than steep takeoffs, although he has made some great 3-4 footers!

One day, we all were at our favorite family summer spot, and after Buddy had his session, I grabbed my longboard and paddled out for a few waves. "Well, look who's followed me into the lineup," I said.  Yup, Buddy swam all the way out to join me for a few waves on the longboard. I put him on the nose, and I stayed at the rear of the board. The only problem was that I was on a 8'6" soft board, and Buddy's rear was directly in my face! He did great, and rode several waves before finally falling off. The soft-top, or soft boards, are the best for Buddy because he can grip the surface.  You can guess that Buddy and I became somewhat noticeable in the lineup, being the only tandem couple that included a dog.

PROFILE

*Buddy fearlessly solos in front of a raging wave*

Recently Buddy really became good so at his surfing that he had all sorts of attention. He got a picture in the local newspaper for ripping up the world famous "Surf Rodeo". Buddy also got to film a pilot working with Amazing Animal Actors for Animal Planet. Buddy starred with their two chimpanzees, Angel and Apollo, in an episode. Buddy did not like the chimps and tried several times to get at them.

Buddy experienced his worst wipeout while training for that show. We were tandem surfing on a 3-4 foot hollow wave and pearled, then Buddy got sucked down and did not surface for several seconds. I thought I had drowned the poor dog, just when he popped up in the turbulent water gasping for air. That is when we found Buddy a life jacket with a handle on the top for safety. Buddy will tolerate several wipeouts before he decides to take a break from surfing, which is usually after an hour or two. Most recently, Buddy filmed a special for Japanese television on unusual animals.

Matthew, Buddy and I enjoy the long summer days with frequent morning or evening surf sessions at our favorite spot, "school house." We have learned how to get Buddy and Matthew on the same wave, each on their own board, riding in together. Matthew is the only kid on the beach that gets to surf with his dog. On weekends, we get quite a bit of attention, ranging from beach walkers to other surfers. The other children boogie boarding just love Buddy. The best quote was from a couple of junior high school boys surfing next to us. One boy commented, "Buddy surfs better than us"!

Buddy has more talents than just surfing, and loves to play games. His favorite game is tag on the play-structure at the beach. He will go round and round, up the stairs, down the different slides, chasing Matthew or Bruce, and nipping at their heels as if to tag them. Matthew plays Little League baseball, and Buddy is a great outfielder. Buddy loves to shag baseballs. Buddy is of course a great swimmer, and can display his amazing balance on a boogie board in a pool. We love to take family hikes to swimming hole or high alpine lakes, and Buddy always enjoys taking a few laps when we reach or destination.

Buddy is truly an amazing dog, a great soul surfer, and certainly a real part of our family.

**PROFILE**

**Bruce Hooker**

Photograph Courtesy of Bruce Hooker

PROFILE

*Buddy rides the wave to the end*

Photo Courtesy of Ed Hepp

*Mugs, patiently waiting for the
gear to hit the sand*

# Surf Dog CHALLENGES

## A FEW REASONS WHY SURFING IS HARDER FOR DOGS

- Dogs can't paddle the board out on their own

- Dogs can't launch the boards on their own (very well, at least)

- Dogs have more hair to get wet and heavy than you do (usually)

- Dogs don't wear wetsuits to keep warm (usually)

- Dogs' toes don't curl like yours, so they don't have the same ability to grip the board or to help with balance

- In general, dogs can't really see where they're going as well as you can

- Dogs get bored if they're alone on a board for too long

- Frisbees and sand crabs can be very distracting

*I've seen dogs ski, skateboard and sail. I've even seen dogs surfing by themselves. Do you have any idea how much free time you must have to train a dog to do that kind of thing? A lot.*

**Ali Landry,**
**Television Host**
**America's Greatest Pets, Wild On E!**

*The first step in a surf dog's evolution:*
*Chasing sticks into the water*

# Surf Dogs on Film

Let's be honest, most people first see dogs surfing in the movies. Of course, as we all know, if something is in the movies then IT CAN BE DONE! Right?

Teaching a dog to surf just because you saw it on film may seem cool, but without humor, trust and fun, the dog isn't going to make that dream a reality. This doesn't mean that the movies aren't onto something.

The following are a few of the flicks, TV shows, and other media that have inspired generations of four-footed thrashers, and even if the dog scenes are short, they're still very cool.  Also, we've included a few surf movies that just inspired us in general.

**Endless Summer II**

**Chairman of the Board**

**Blue Crush**

**Lilo & Stitch**

**North Shore**

**Billabon Odyssey**

**Step Into Liquid**

## Endless Summer II

For almost three decades the Endless Summer was the only "real" surf movie around. Two guys travel the world to find the best surf spots, meet great surfers, and find the perfect wave. The Endless Summer II: The Journey Continues was a great follow-up by original director Bruce Brown, done in the same documentary style that reveals the soul of surfing. Of course, they meet some great surf dogs along the way.

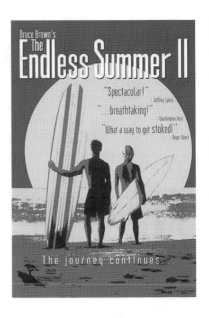

*Surf Movie Rating: High*
*Surf Dog Scene: Yes*

## Chairman of the Board

This movie never received raves from the critics, for the obvious reason that they would have lost their jobs. Comedian Carrot Top plays a surfer-inventor trying to make rent who ends up taking his "skills" to the boardroom after he inherits the firm. Hilarity ensues... not! The movie's redeeming feature is a shot of a dog surfing, reinforcing our belief that the surf dog was actually the movie's real star.

*Surf Movie Rating: Low*
*Surf Dog Scene: Yes*

## Blue Crush

This is a very entertaining movie, and it brought a lot of people a real appreciation of the challenges it takes to be a surfer, especially a female surfer. These challenges include: Respect, money and competition. Of course, there are some flaws in the plot, but the filming is beautiful, the professional surfers are real, pro-surfer Sanoe Lake has a lead role, and heck, it makes everyone watching it want to hit the beach.

Originally called, "Surf Girls of Maui," the movie stars Kate Bosworth, who tries to deal with the three challenges mentioned above while helping to raise her teenage sister and get over a near-death surfing experience while she  prepares for the biggest surf contest of her life. Dog surf shots in the beginning and during credits show the surf culture lifestyle.

*Surf Movie Rating: High*
*Surf Dog Scene: Yes*

*Stitch, Nani and Lilo catch a wave in Hawaii*

## Lilo & Stitch

Does making hundreds of millions of dollars and setting new box office records for an animated film actually make a movie worth watching? In this case, it does. Lilo & Stitch is a fantastic family movie from Disney, but more importantly, it's a good surf dog film. This is because runaway alien prisoner/war machine "Stitch" comes to Hawaii to escape his evil captors, impersonates a dog (a very ugly one), and is adopted from the pound by local girl Lilo. Lilo is being raised by her sister, who tries to keep custody of Lilo while holding down a steady job. Stitch loves surfing, though he hates water, and the film embraces surf culture, island culture, and the meaning of family. Plus there's humor, action, adventure... and surfing.

***Surf Movie Rating: High***
***Alien Imitating a Surf Dog Scene: Yes***

*There are quite a number of people that have taught their dogs to surf. These, generally, are people that surf themselves and not movie trainers. When we need a surfing dog we try to locate someone with one. Those dogs usually don't do too many other tricks because their owners aren't interested in 'training,' just surfing.*

**Rob, Critters of the Cinema**

## North Shore

This is another fictional surfer movie with a real surfer spirit. Actually, the theme repeated over and over is not to surf for fame and fortune but as a "soul surfer." The star of the film comes to the legendary North Shore from

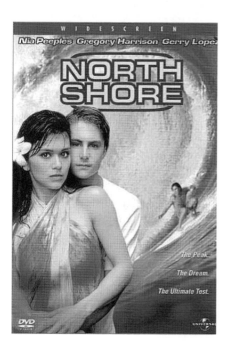

a few wins in Arizona's wave pools to compete with the pros, but meets Nia Peeples and others, including real life surfers Derek Ho and Mark Foo, and learns a thing or two.

The best lines are:

Rick: "So this is where you work, Turtle?"

Turtle: "Only when da surf's bad. Cause' when da surf's good, nobody works!"

***Surf Movie Rating: High***
***Surf Dog Scene: No***

## Billabong Odyssey

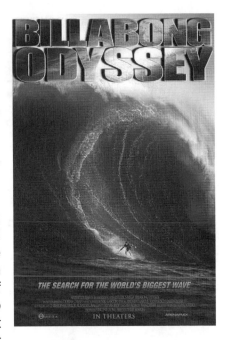

The movie's tagline is

"The search for the world's biggest wave."

When they say big, they mean BIG.

The industry's best big wave surfers go around the globe to find the biggest wave they can handle. Since some of these waves are up to 70 feet high, a height from which you wouldn't want to fall even if it were into cotton, the quest is awesome to behold.

The film is an action sports documentary covering six continents and 18 months, and if you're serious about surfing, and want to see how far you could go, it's a must-see.

Yes, you also might suspect that there is a classical literature reference to Homer's epic work, "The Odyssey," recounting Odysseus' twenty-year journey to return home after the Trojan War.

Apparently he ran into some big waves too.

*Surf Movie Rating: High*
*Surf Dog Scene: No*

## Step Into Liquid

"No special effects.
No stuntmen.
No stereotypes.
No other feeling comes close."

By the son of Bruce Brown (Endless Summer), Dana.

If you're not a professional surfer, judge, or photographer, then you will rarely get to see the full, and beautiful, spectrum of the surfing scene as you can in this film.

Cinematically awe-inspiring, it travels around the world to show you surfers in extreme conditions, with extreme conditions (think paralysis), or going to extremes to make the most of conditions (like surfing behind the wakes of oil tankers).

This film is inspirational, to say the least.

*Surf Movie Rating: High*

*Surf Dog Scene: Yes*

*Wavefest logos and posters of surf film nights and other events. Illustrations courtesy of Wavefest.*

## Surfing Thrills & Spills

Oddball Film + Video is a place I interned at for a few months, probably back in '98. It is a classic warehouse in the Mission District of San Francisco, with literally tens of thousands of 16mm films from floor to ceiling. I think the original intention of these films were for library and classroom use, so many of them featured basic, bland narration. I spent hours cleaning films with such titles as "Electricity: Be Safe," and "Common Grey Squirrels."

When programming the '01 festival, I was allowed to sift through a few surf films in the archive, and was given permission to show two of them, one being "Surfing Thrills & Spills" (1939). I chose it for the reasons of age, history, and humor.

However, "Surfing Thrills & Spills" was so old that it used title cards instead of cheesy narration. The black & white film featured surf stylings by a young Hawaiian in the Honolulu surf. Of course the surfboard is ancient, obviously pre-dating any fiberglass/foam creations.

At one point, a dog hops on the board for a few spins with its owner. The audience usually gets a chuckle out of this, as it is definitely pretty cute. But then the owner surprisingly falls off, and the dog is left to charge the wave on its own, and it succeeds in taking it pretty far! At this point, the audience usually bursts into cheers for the hot-dogging pooch.

It's pretty cool that a film of such age and innocence can still attract and entertain an audience. Definitely says something about the allure of surfers to surf films, and our affinity towards man's best friend.

Brian Musial,
WAVEFEST Surf Film Festival

About WAVEFEST: WAVEFEST is a surf film festival which was conceived in the Summer of 2001 with another out of work friend. They wanted to bring surf films (which is such a big part of surf culture/tradition) back into movie theaters, except with a twist.

# The Surf Dog of Santa Cruz

The award-nominated Waxfoot Surf Show is a half hour weekly TV show on local Santa Cruz channel 27, co-produced by Michael Congdon and wife Annie, who shoot, edit and put together the whole thing.

The show is about surfing, before work surfing, after school surfing, big waves, little waves, contests, events, beginners and pros, women and kids, and old timers, plus ocean-oriented community stuff, families at the beach, and anything unusual.

One day Michael and Annie were shooting some video in front of Jack O'Neill's house. That's when they first saw Skateboard Mike and his surfing dog, Bailey. Skateboard

Mike is a really nice guy who lives in the San Francisco Bay Area and Bailey is his seven year old Beagle. They come to Santa Cruz because he says "It's the only place Bailey likes to surf."

Photographs and Video Courtesy of the Waxfoot Surf Show

# Eddy the Eco-Dog

Can a surf dog be a role model for children across the Universe? Eddy the Eco-Dog certainly is.

In 1991, Lorane Poersch, then an international broker of post-consumer recycled plastic, was in the middle of writing a proposal to present to a British corporation when she had a sudden brainstorm. Her unexpected idea was to create a fun-loving character that would make kids giggle and kindle their curiosity to discover. Because of this epiphany Eddy the Eco-Dog was born on the planet "Chachachawowa."

Lorane found inspiration for Eddy the Eco-Dog from spending time in Hawaii, stirred by the surfers' love for adventure and respect for nature and her experience in the rugged wilderness of the Canadian Arctic with a silly old yellow lab named "Mikey."

Explains Lorane, "Eddy the Eco-Dog is not your average canine. Raised by intergalactic investigators, Eddy is a star-surfing, fun-loving, dogbone-pizza-eating pooch equipped with an intergalactic surfboard and an uncontrollable curiosity. He will always be the first dog up on stage for Karaoke. Eddy's turning things upside down as his curiosity and taste for adventure get him and his pals into every predicament imaginable as they discover wonders from earth to their home planet of Chachachawowa and beyond."

Eddy has an eclectic group of friends who

are rough around the edges and sometimes misunderstood by others, but Eddy is loyal to all of them: Lixxy is a tomboy with a mondo crush on Eddy; Yolanda is the owner of the local diner who gives advice and has an opinion on everything; and Rosco is a grumpy old alligator hermit who lives out in the woods.

Eddy the Eco-Dog, a surfer dude with an attitude, surfed to fame in his own webcartoon series: "Online! Unleashed!" at "http://www.KidsWebTv.com" and with international broadcast exposure on two kids' cable networks. The webcartoon series has been widely recognized throughout the world with loyal viewers from around the globe such as Japan, Argentina and Germany.

# The Loch Ness Surf Dog Of New Zealand

Traveler Steve Castellotti describes his first sighting of a surf dog, an experience that he felt was as exciting as possibly seeing the legendary Loch Ness Monster.

"It was the third day of a motorcycle tour around the North Island of New Zealand, when I took a Ferry across the Bay of Islands to the Victorian city of Russell. Once the country's capital and later known for its seedy reputation as a den for lawless adventurers and wild women, 'Romantic Russell' is now a major tourist destination -appreciated as much for its quiet charm and natural beauty as its sordid history.

I was relaxing in the shade at a picnic table near the water's edge when the sound of a speedboat passing by snapped me out of my book. Losing all interest in the novel, I lunged for my camera as a most extraordinary scene developed. Tearing through the quiet coastal waters, a man was taking his dog out for a different kind of walk on a sunny afternoon. A line attached to the speed boat was towing a body-board, on top of which was perched a small dog wearing a wetsuit.

Casual as can be, the dog kept its balance as the man whipped and turned back and forth along the shoreline. Tourists began pointing and remarking to each other as a smile spread across their faces. The dog seemed pretty happy too. The wind in its face and the smell of the surf must have been far better than struggling to lean out of any car window. I have to admit it looked like such fun I wished it was me on that board.

Photographs Courtesy of Steve Castellotti

After a few runs back and forth the man pulled up to the water's edge, with the amazing surfing dog drifting alongside him. With a splash the dog jumped into the water and swam over to the waiting arms of its proud owner."

Seeing the true surf dog spirit, Steve came to this conclusion, "On the road to becoming a true surf dog, every canine has to work its way up through the basics. From balancing on the board to judging the current and riding out that wave, there's one thing that distinguishes the novice from the master: Style."

Loch Ness Monster, beat that!

# Surfer Dog:
# The Novel

Surf dogs are so popular that they even have their own literature. Author Elizabeth Spurr's book SURFER DOG is a case in point. This book, written for ages 8-12, is a great example of the nurturing bond of friendship between person, dog, and board.

Says Elizabeth on how she came to create SURFER DOG:

"While living on the oceanfront in Cayucos, California, I began watching a man and his dog, a Labrador, who surfed every evening near sunset. They would swim out to a large rock and wait until a good wave approached, then dive into the water. As the man paddled his board to meet the wave, the dog kept up with him.

I followed the pair wave after wave; the dog seemed to have an uncanny sense of timing. He would catch the wave like an expert body surfer; rising to the crest, and dropping at exactly the right moment.

Fascinated by the dog's love of waves, and his ability to ride them, I began my book SURFER DOG, in which a dog shows his young master which waves to take."

**The following is a hang-ten excerpt from Elizabeth Spurr's best-selling novel, SURFER DOG.**

" I follow Blackie, paddling way beyond the breakline. The dog swims in circles while I straddle the board. All of a sudden he whimpers and noses seaward. Sure enough, a big old set of swells is moving in.

Blackie drifts over the first and second swell, then paddles like fury toward shore. I do the same. We both catch wave number three right on the peak and sail into shore past a whole line of boards.

I see my chance to do a little fancy work. I throw a couple of quick slashes and end with a frontside aerial, which I stick.

When I finally sink into a foot of water, one of the guys puts up a thumb and calls, "Grr-eat ride!" But I see he's looking at the dog."

*Right: Cover of the novel,*
*"Surfer Dog."*

# Surfer Dog

# Dog

ELIZABETH SPURR

# Favorite Surf Dog Beach Activities

- **Surfing**

- **Checking out other dogs**

- **Playing in water**

- **Chasing Frisbees**

- **Chasing sticks**

- **Chasing gulls**

- **Chasing crabs (or cars)**

- **Sniffing everything in area**

- **Walking on beach towel while wet and covered in sand**

- **Building inverted sand castles (also known as 'digging a big hole in the ground')**

*Above: Building "inverted" sand castles,
this one goes all the way to Tahiti*

Photograph courtesy of Tahiti Tourisme

# How To Train Your Dog To Do New Skills

Some dogs are natural surfers. No I don't mean left-pawed or goofy-footed or something like that, but are just born to surf. Yes, there are dogs that can be happily taught anything, but there are others who would rather be in a ballet than balanced on a wave in the water.

Photograph Courtesy of Carolyn Press Mckenzie, Amazing Animals

Whatever type of dog owns you, take a moment to ponder. Is your dog physically suited to surfing (i.e. a British Bulldog could potentially just sink!)

Most importantly - will your dog enjoy it?

### 3 simple rules of training

- Set yourself up for success.
- Always end a session on a high.
- Never loose sight of the fact that this is supposed to be FUN!!

You may be lucky enough to have a dog that jumps straight onto your 5'6" and hangs 20 with style all the way to shore the first time out. In general, for most dogs though, surfing can feel very unnatural and if you throw them in at the deep end, as it were, they may just panic.

## Set yourself up for success

Open the lines of communication between you and your pooch.   Start your training with baby steps on old terra firma and take the sure and steady approach - your dog will be eternally grateful. Like any athlete your dog needs to build up to that big one. If you communicate well, making sure he understands what is being asked of him, you'll be there in no time.

## Step 1. Positive reinforcement

 Do you remember your biology teacher explaining the "Pavlov Theory?" When Pavlov rang his bell, his dogs would start salivating in anticipation of food. Well, in a around about way this is the basis for teaching your dog anything.

Food motivation, harnessed correctly via positive reinforcement, could lead your plight to tremendous success. It's basically something we fancy trainers call conditioned response training.

You will need:
- A "positive reinforcer". A clicker, a whistle or just a word of praise like "good" or "yes". I like to use a clicker as its distinct sound lets the dog know exactly when he's got it right.

- A bum bag full of diced frankfurter or whatever else tickles his fancy. This is just a token reward so make sure the treats are diced nice and small, we don't want your dog to sink like a slab of concrete because their stomach is ful. Of course, many dogs will work well for a pat or a toy, so see how you get on.
- Good timing. The most important part of conditioned response training is timing. The idea is to reinforce the behaviors that you desire at the exact moment when they happen. For example, when Haggis gets it right I click he clicker, so she knows she has nailed it and that a treat or a head pat will follow.

## Step 2. Sit/Stay and working to a mark.

Choose some command words. Say them, mean them, and always follow through. Dogs understand consistency.

This is a good time to introduce the all-important "suction-grip bath mat". This mat is hugely significant to safe surfboard training; it will give your pooch confidence. Slipping and falling off due to lack of grip can set you back, way back!

We are also going to use the mat as a mark to work too.

## Step 3. Establish some balance

This is where you need to realize the handyman/woman in yourself. Look around for things that move. A wheelbarrow, tea trolley, computer cart or pram could suffice. I would say a skateboard is not preferable at this stage, as it's too low to the ground and therefore too easy to jump off. Remember you're trying to set yourselves up for success.

Place the matt on top of the wheelbarrow or trolley, making sure that it will not slip or fall off accidentally.

Now, secure the rig so that it doesn't move at first. Ask your best friend to hop up onto the makeshift surfboard. I normally use the command "get up."

Once they are on top, you can build their confidence and balance by slowly moving the rig. They should start becoming comfortable after a few tries, at which point you can go a bit faster, or rock it gently up and down. Don't rush the process, the point is not to scare them.

Dogs learn quickly, and after practicing on this "dry land" surfboard, the transition to a board on water should be much easier and faster.

### Carolyn Press Mckenzie

### Head Trainer/Coordinator Animal Actors NZ

# Animal Actors NZ est 1998
# Wellington, NZ

**Carolyn and Jim Press Mckenzie** live on their 14 acre Animal Sanctuary and Training Facility just 35 minutes from the heart of Wellington. In addition to providing the highest quality performance animals for film and television, they offer a rehabilitation and rescue center for injured birds and animals.

Head Trainer/Coordinator Carolyn has 6yrs film and television experience, 17 years as a qualified Veterinary Nurse; She specialises in Animal Behaviour problems and is currently studying for a certificate in Animal Welfare Investigations. Carolyn's skills begin with script breakdowns, then casting – from White Tigers to Giant Moths, we can source anything – the end result, turning the Directors vision into reality.

Credits include:

| | | |
|---|---|---|
| Seed Productions | JUST PATTERSONS | dog |
| Wilco | Gallagher | dogs,cat |
| 3 foot 6 | LORD OF THE RINGS III | pick up – farm animals |
| Wilco | WRIGHTSONS | cow, sheep |
| Touchdown Prod | WORLDS BEST | eels, cat fish |
| Wilco | TAB | horse |
| BBC | THE LOST WORLD | tarantula, monkey, carthorses, dogs, parrot, chickens, pigs |
| Cowgirl Productions | SNAKESKIN | lead dog, eels, sheep, goat. |
| Nine eye Productions | EVENT 16 | rearing horse, cart horses, cat |
| Cloud 9 Productions | THE TRIBE series II & III | lead dog, rats, horses, spiders, farm animals |
| Cloud 9 Productions | THE TRIBE | lead dog, unicorn pony, doves, butterflies |

# The Surf Dog Making it in Commercials & Television

*Bottom, this page: Haggis the surfing stunt dog, on the set of a commercial with Amazing Animals of New Zealand.*

*Top Right: A quick session on a moving boogie board helps to gain Haggis' concentration.*

*Bottom Right: Haggis hanging ten (or twenty) on the set.*

Photographs Courtesy of Carolyn Press Mckenzie, Amazing Animals

# Training Your Dog, Again and Again

In the every day process of "training our dog" we need to remember one vitally important point. Training IS an every day occurrence.

Walking into a dog training class is merely an hour of pointers meant to help the OWNER work with his dog, and the dog socialize with other dogs. The real meat and potatoes training happens when the owner(s) are CONSISTENT and practice daily, enforcing and rewarding positive behaviors.

If you want your dog to exhibit ANY behavior, make PRACTICE FUN, and reward OFTEN. I promise you, that then you will get the best from both you and your best friend!

Lyn Richards

Doglogic Canine Resource Center

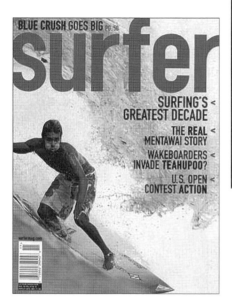

Courtesy of © Surfer Magazine

*It's cool to take your dog surfing because dog's guarantee a good time. The waves might be crap, but with your dog, well, you're going to have a fun session. Plus, dogs break down a lot of social barriers. You can meet lots of interesting people. Let's face it, a cool dog is the ultimate hottie magnet. I've seen a Golden Retriever surf down at an infamous point break in Baja that was getting rides that were at least 100 yards long.*

*The equipment you really need are sunglasses; the dog has to be wearing a cool pair of shades.*

**Scott Bass**
**Surfer magazine**

# Great Moves the Surf Dog Cannot Do

Regardless of how much training they do, and how naturally talented they are, there are some surfing moves that a dog just can't make. Take heart, though. If you show them to your dog often enough, they might pick up a trick or two that will surprise you.

*Photographs this page and opposite Courtesy of © Roxy*

# Great Move the Surf Dog Can Do

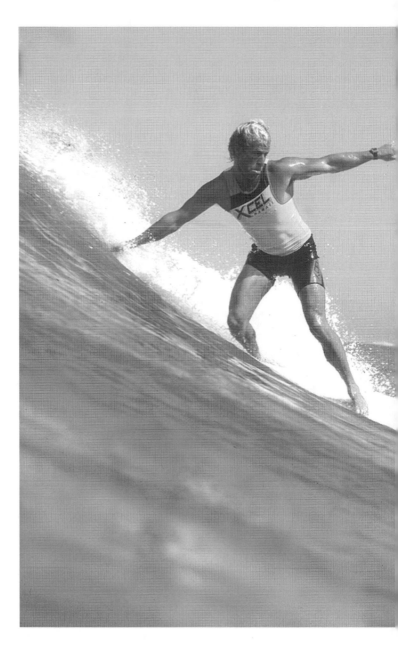

*Above: Mugs and Ed, getting ready to hit the waves*

*Below: Mugs coasting in the prone position*

Photographs Courtesy of Ed Hepp

# Tails from the Nose: Mugs & Ed

I was born and mostly grew up in Southeastern Pennsylvania where I had very little exposure to the ocean (think Jersey Shore, boardwalk, big hair--I was a child of the'80s) and the recreational opportunities it provides, so surfing was one of the farthest things from my mind as a kid. My passions were with sports like baseball and soccer, but above all I was enthralled with fishing and the real connection it afforded me with the natural world around us. I've had what some might consider an unhealthy obsession with flyfishing since I was about 10 years old. This, along with plentiful snow for skiing, is a big part of what brought me to Oregon, with its multitude of mountains, rivers and lakes, in 1992. The last thing I ever thought Oregon would introduce me to was surfing, but surfing has turned out to be one of the biggest contributions to my life that life Oregon has provided. I first paddled out on a board in 1994 at the age of 25 and I haven't looked back since. Surfing most of Oregon is a real wilderness experience and I tend to seek out the spots that magnify this aspect. There are a few places on the North Oregon coast that require beautiful hikes through stands of old growth forest to reach what are often times world class waves. Sometimes the hike itself, and may be a few salmonberries or chanterelles along the way, ends up being the only reward, but that's the price we pay for the times it's on and most everybody else is surfing crowded closeouts in front of a parking lot. So now I'm 34, I've seen parts of the world I'd never dreamed I'd visit, I have aspirations for even more travel to even farther corners of the globe, and I'm in better shape, both physically and mentally, than was ten years ago. It's great to be a surfer.

Mugs is a direct descendant of dogs I had while growing up. His great grandfather, Red, was a golden retriever that my father and I trained for field trialing back in the 70's. He was an amazing dog and the experience I gained while training him has been invaluable in my relationships with dogs since then. A few generations of both intentional and unintentional breeding, including the addition of a little Labrador Retriever blood, led to the litter from which I picked Mugs. It was fortuitous timing for the litter to have been born when I was ready and prepared to raise a puppy. For years I'd wanted a dog for a companion, but my work schedule made it impossible for me to commit the time I knew was necessary to do it the way I felt was right. A switch to free-lancing opened the door for me and subsequently Mugs was born. The fact that he was descendent from our family dogs made it even better; he is like a family member, himself.

Mugs goes just about everywhere with me, and the beach is simply dog heaven so of course he's always there when I am. Fortunately, Oregon is a bit more spacious and a lot less developed than places like Southern California, so Mugs is usually able to run free, especially at the beach.

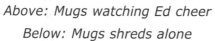

*Above: Mugs watching Ed cheer*
*Below: Mugs shreds alone*

In my opinion, there's nothing sadder than a dog on a leash at the beach. I almost always make my surf check while simultaneously hucking the frisbee for Mugs to sky out for and preform his usual bag of show-off tricks. He knows when people notice him and he can be real ham about it. He's got a lot of style, though, and definitely deserves the attention. He was once doing his frisbee tricks at dog beach in Oceanbeach (S.D.) and ended up in a book about golden retrievers. It was a chance meeting with the photographer Denver Bryan, who added Mugs to his book "Golden Rules."

**PROFILE**

I always make several frisbee throws out into the surf and he charges in after them without hesitation. This has contributed greatly to his comfort level while surfing. He knows how to get up over a wall of whitewater and how to use that same whitewater to assist his swim back into shore. Of course I'm always mindful of his limits and would never put him in a situation that was beyond his abilities to cope with. Not only would this be dangerous, but it would be the surest way to lose his trust and destroy his confidence and desire to continue his love affair with the water. When he was a puppy he would often times try to follow me out into the line up. I could always paddle a lot faster than he could swim, though, and once I got far enough away or he got far enough out that the waves were washing over him he'd head back in. This always made me feel like he'd really enjoy being out there and that one day I'd eventually try putting him on a board to see how he would do.

Any dog who trusts his human and has confidence and skill swimming in the surf zone, provided the right equipment and conditions, can easily learn how to surf. The most important thing is to keep it fun for them. If the dog gets dunked and/or looks afraid of the situation, take him in to the beach and do something else that he enjoys. It's always better to finish any kind of training situation with the dog wanting to do more than it is to push things the point where he is no longer having a good time.

With Mugs, I just laid him on the board, got him stabilized, held him steady so he'd relax and pushed him gently into the wave. I thought he'd jump right off at first, but he stayed on. He seemed to love it.

PROFILE

The photos here show Mugs in his first ever surf session. He rode a few waves, including the first one I pushed him into, all the way to the beach, or basically where the wave washed out into shin-deep water. We missed the first ride because I hadn't reloaded the film in the camera. I don't think I really expected him to do it on the first try. Jay, on the beach with the camera, probably would have missed the shot anyway, we were laughing so hard. It was the pinnacle moment of stoke on a five week road trip stretching the lengths of Oregon, California and Baja that was pitifully lacking in decent swell. And this little cove in Baja Norte gave us one last chance to surf semi-warm water in very clean, but pathetically small surf. It proved to be the perfect learning spot for Mugs; about knee to waist high and slowly peeling. We got the film loaded and went back out for more. On the next wave he got kind of turned around, laying sideways with his feet curled up on either side of the board and looking back at me. I threw my hands up in the air and hooted at him, then the wave sectioned and wiped him out. This didn't discourage him, though, and he enthusiastically returned to the line up for a few more rides. The toughest thing for him was the hard, fiberglass deck. He wasn't comfortable standing so he'd lay down kind of tensed up with his nails digging in at first. I think a soft top or some sort of padded surface on the deck would make any dog much more comfortable and help him relax.

**PROFILE**

As far as safety goes, with regards to the physical characteristics of the surfing environment, the depth of the water is of no real consequence. Once the water is to your thighs, the dog is swimming. I'd be most concerned about a situation where a wave was breaking hard over shallow water, especially over rocks or a reef. Don't put the dog in a situation where it's loss of control would likely cause it harm, either physical or psychological. And make sure you're as close to shore as you need to be for your dog to easily swim in at will. Mugs is a strong swimmer and gets a lot of exercise, so he can probably swim farther than me. Know the dog's limits. If he's going to stay on the board, he has to trust you.

I've never used food as a reward for anything, nor would I ever deny it as a form of punishment. The greatest reward I can bestow upon Mugs is praise and an enthusiastic expression of satisfaction. He loves to please and I give him the opportunity to do so with activities that provide him with both physical and mental stimulation and challenge. At the end of the day, he's happy to eat his bowl full of dry nuggets and he's healthier for it, too.

As with cars and boats and any other type of vehicle, a dog is pretty much just along for the ride. They're not pumping down the line thinking "Oo, I'm gonna bash the lip on that next section coming up," but they're still having a damn good time. You push the dog into the wave and he goes where the board takes him. If he figures out how to and/or decides he wants to stay on the board, he will. The more positive the experience is for the dog, the more likely he's going to want to do it. If he doesn't want to do it, he's not going to do it. If he does it, he must love it.

 PROFILE

## Ed Hepp

©Edward J. Hepp, III

Photographs Courtesy of Ed Hepp

*Mugs demonstrating perfect canine board placement
for balance, confidence and maximum attitude*

# Dog Placement on the Board

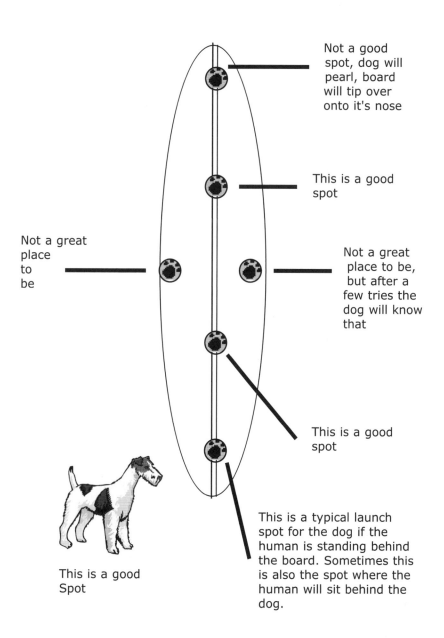

Not a good spot, dog will pearl, board will tip over onto it's nose

This is a good spot

Not a great place to be

Not a great place to be, but after a few tries the dog will know that

This is a good spot

This is a good Spot

This is a typical launch spot for the dog if the human is standing behind the board. Sometimes this is also the spot where the human will sit behind the dog.

# Salute to Rocky, an International Surf Dog Legend

**Wavescape Editor Steve Pike writes an obituary for Cape Town, South Africa's most famous surf dog, Rocky the Boxer, who died of old age**

It's a sad day for surfing. Rocky, the infamous surfing boxer dog, passed away early this week. He had lived a rich and colourful life, and died at the grand old age of 14.

The irony is that as that two days after he died, a massive winter storm hit the Cape and the swell jacked up to levels unsurpassed this year.

Rocky and his owner Rob, dubbed by the Glen Beach crew as Admiral Pointdexter (he prefers to be called Rob), were inseparable. If Rob was surfing somewhere deep in the kelp off Soetwater, the Kom or the Factory, you could be certain that Rocky was lurking about chasing kelp lice or chewing body boarders' fins on the beach.

If Rob went out at night to a bar, or a friend's house, Rocky was always in tow. On surf trips in other people's cars, you had to have a really persuasive argument to leave Rocky behind. Dog hairs and drool all over the back seat and windows was insufficient reason to deny Rocky his right to come along.

If you wore a uniform, and Rocky checked you out, you were history. He was obsessed with uniforms. In a split second, Rocky would be transformed from a peace-loving, beach-chilling surf hound into a snarling snapping beast, jowls flopping up and down like jelly, spittle spattering the car windows.

Perhaps this strange quirk resulted from the time Rocky was savaged by an alpha male baboon in his frivolous youth. A pack of baboons must have grown tired of being chased up and down the mountain at 365s. One day, the yellow-eyed leader decided it was payback time.

Rocky chased a member of the troop into some bushes, snarling and bucking in Rocky style. His owner claims vehemently that Rocky wouldn't have known what to do once he caught anything. The occasional bodyboarder or petrol attendant might testify otherwise.

Meanwhile, the alpha male baboon had circled back around the fracas and, with his back to the ocean, blocked Rocky's path to his beloved master, and attacked with a ferocity that only fang-bared baboons exhibit.

Rob heard the screams of pain, and with a bloodcurdling cry managed to scare off the baboon.

Disemboweled and ripped apart, Rocky escaped death by a whisker and the swift work of a skilled vet.

Rocky was a true surf dog, and lived for the ocean. Rocky, we salute you. Let's hope that dog heaven is populated by plenty of policemen and nurses.

# Surf Dog Safety

When taking your dog to surf, keep in mind some of the unique challenges both you and your canine tandem partner are going to face. There are a variety of situations that a mature human can handle and a dog can't, or at least not very well. These include:

- **Rocks**
- **Reefs**
- **Waves**
- **Inattention**
- **Leashes**
- **Floating & Swimming**
- **Cold**
- **Marine Fauna**

## Rocks

Small stones are generally not a problem for dogs, though they may hurt a human's feet from time to time. The real challenge is in areas with large boulders that line the shore or create a break or seawall. When dogs walk out on these they can easily slip in and get sucked down into the spaces between and below the rocks. The average dog is going to have a hard time climbing its way out of such a situation.

Dogs in the water also need to be careful. A dog on a board heading towards large rocks has no way to paddle and turn the board around. Its only choice is to jump off and let the board go.

## Reefs

Having your dog crash into a reef is just way too scary to think about. Fur is not the best protection against coral's razor sharp edges. If reefs are very close to the surface, you really don't want your dog surfing, walking, or swimming over them.

## Waves

Regardless of a dog's water skills, the one thing of which you can be certain is that it is not a good idea to either put them on a very large wave or take them into the curl. In fact, taking a dog in the curl is NOT RECOMMENDED.

Despite this advice, if you decide it's worth the risk, try to keep the dog low, use a soft-top board,

*Above: A tired dog underwater can weigh as much as a heavy stone. Here, legendary high surf lifeguard Brian Keaulana trains for big wave action with underwater "rock running." From the film, "Billabong Odyssey" © 2003 Arenaplex*

put them in a lifejacket, have a friend watch as a spotter, and if you've got one, use a collar with a radio-locator. Of course, if you don't do any of these things and just go for it the pup still might survive. That would be one lucky dog.

## A few other saftey tips.

## Inattention

Your dog on the beach can take care of themselves, at least if it's a true beach dog. Your dog on a board is˙ another story. That dog is your responsibility, which means they are trusting you to watch their back at all times. If you get too distracted by Van's massive snaps, Abubo in the pipe, or a hottie on the sand, you might have to do a Baywatch and rescue your canine surfing buddy from some unexpected, though real, drama.

## Leashes

In surfing, a leash is a cord attached to the surfer's ankle and the board that prevents the board from drifting away from a surfer in the water. Leashes are really, really good for you. You should wear one. Leashes are not really, really good for a dog in the water, at least that is the general surfing consensus. The logic is that a lease could stop a dog from swimming effectively, or worse, could get wrapped around their legs, paws or neck.

*If the leash is caught on the dog, it may as well be a rope and anchor*

Don't worry too much about the leash that you're wearing getting caught around the dog. If that happens it shouldn't be too difficult take it off your ankle and undo the loops before the situation gets serious.

## Floating & Swimming

We've already talked about this, but if the dog isn't a good swimmer they should not be on a surfboard. If they're on a board it is guaranteed

*Above & Left: If you take your dog into deep or turbulent water, a doggy life vest is highly recommended.*

*One of the most respected names in canine Personal Safety Devices (PSD) is Ruff Wear*

Photographs courtesy of Ruff Wear, © Ruff Wear

that at some point in time they're going to fall in the water, and a wet drowning panicked dog is a lot heavier than you think.

"But dogs don't panic," you say? True dat, most of the time they're pretty cool when in the drink. But if they get a little confused or tired or stuck on a piece of kelp, floating is not their strong point, and the barking thing is not very informative. Make sure your dog is a strong swimmer.

## Cold

Cold dogs can get tired, lethargic, and unable to swim. Keep an eye out and make sure your dog is not losing too much heat. Says surfer Bruce

*Below: It may never be too cold for you to surf, but your dog can't put on a wetsuit. Here, Australia's Layne Beachley, five-time Association of Surfing Professionals World Champion, has the right idea on how to keep warm. From the film, "Billabong Odyssey" © 2003 Arenaplex*

Hooker about celebrity surf dog Buddy, "When Buddy is tired, or finished, he shows hesitancy. He usually runs into warm dry sand and try to roll in it to get warm. The water where we surf is often between 60-68 degrees, and he does get cold after about an hour, except on hot summer days. Buddy will take a break, and want to go again later."

## Fauna

Not the girl's name, we're talking about the animals that live in the water. Given the chance, some of these little sea-loving creatures could play real havoc with a dog, and vice versa. You might want to surf in jellyfish, but leave the dog out of it. Sharks don't scare you, no worries, but leave the dog out of it. Barracudas, urchins, morays, rays, sharp shells in the sand... you get the point.

You're there for the fun and the excitement, the dog it there for the fun. Other animals trying to make them lunch may be exciting but it is not a dog's idea of fun.

Image this page courtesy of Surfing Australia

# "Who watches out for dog safety in all of those surf films?"

The answer is the American Humane Association's (AHA) Film and Television Unit. For over 123 years, it has been the mission of the American Humane Association (AHA) to protect animals and children from cruelty, abuse and neglect. In a recent four years period, the American Humane Association (AHA) has monitored the humane care and treatment of tens of thousands of animals that have appeared in almost 3,000 films, television shows, and commercials under AHA's jurisdiction.

Internationally, outside of AHA's jurisdiction, a network of local humane organizations monitor many of the hundreds of American productions filming in their regions by utilizing AHA's Guidelines for the Safe Use of Animals in Filmed Media. The result is a much safer environment for pet stars. This environment is the result of AHA's 60 years of advocacy on behalf of animal actors and the film industry's decision in 1980 to voluntarily grant AHA an official oversight role, and contrasts sharply from the days when wire-tripping horses and other cruelties were frequently found in filming.

The AHA works collaboratively with the film industry to achieve these goals and to see that the highest degree of safety and humane treatment is available. In fact, AHA guidelines are stricter than any federal or state regulations. The results of any AHA investigations are always made public. American Humane Association publishes information about the work of its Film Unit on its website www.ahafilm.org, in AHA's publications, and in a variety of print and electronic media.

Hollywood has a rich history of animal stories. Positive and important messages about animals in our society have reached millions of Americans through the adventures of such animal actors as Rin-Tin-Tin, Lassie, and Babe the pig. The American Humane Association is proud of its work with the film industry making sure these animal actors can tell their stories in a safe and humane environment.

# Tails from the Nose: Dee & Sunde

My dog Dee has tried surfing with me exactly two times. Each time resulted in her almost drowning, followed by an embarrassing rescue attempt by me. The first time she was about nine months old when she caught sight of me paddling into the beach after surfing for the day. She sprinted down the sand and straight into the head-high shore break, apparently assuming she'd be able to run on water like she could on land. She disappeared under the surface instantly. I caught a glimpse of her in the water with her spooked eyes opened wide right before the wave washed over her.

Dee looks very much like a brown-haired cinder block with legs. Having her jump into the ocean is the equivalent of a solid brick being thrown into deep water. My heart stopped as I envisioned her anchored right to the ocean floor by her own weight. Fortunately, the wave passed and amazingly there she was, running in place, with only her eyes and nose above the water, trying her best to dog paddle over to me.

"Come here Dee Dee!" I shouted with relief, "Come on!" But try as I might I couldn't paddle over to her before another wave pushed her up to its peak, and then sucked her right down the other side. "Damn." I muttered. She was nowhere in sight. With no other viable option, I manically paddled to the shore, only to find Dee laying on the sand surrounded be a semi-circle of surfers. She looked like a half-drowned seal pup. I ran over to her, fully prepared to perform doggy CPR, when she leapt to her feet and began kissing me joyfully. Fine as always, lucky dog.

The second time she went into the water was on a point break off of a rocky jetty. Dee followed me along the big slippery boulders, picking her way delicately like a mountain goat. I jumped off a rock and paddled towards the lineup, assuming she would wait patiently on the rocks. When I looked back over my shoulder she was balanced precariously on a slanted slab of cement, barking and crying.

"Go back Dee Dee!" I shouted, "Go back!" Instead, what she seemed to hear was, "Blah blah, Dee Dee! Blah blah!" and then began plotting her way closer to the water. She couldn't see the set wave swelling up behind her. I cursed, knowing I was about to witness my beloved dog get swept up in the sea and pummeled violently on the rocks . As fate would have it, Dee turned around just in time to see the wave right before it yanked her off her feet, totally enveloping her.

"DEE DEE!" I screamed, alerting the entire lineup to the very panicked lady paddling frantically towards the rocks. I tried to I reach her as fast as I could, and released the leash from my ankle and let my board go. I swam the last bit of distance to the jetty and climbed onto one of the rocks. I peered over it, only to find Dee swimming frenetically in a whirlpool while trying to find a foothold to pull herself up out of the water. I lay down on my stomach, reached over, grabbed her by the collar, and dragged her to safety on the jetty.

Dee shook herself and followed me back to the beach - wet, tired and miserable. When we got

Painting by Sunde White ©

there I saw that my longboard had crashed into a little girl's sand castle, thus alerting everyone to the spectacle of a woman stomach-down on a rock, fishing for her drowning dog. Eyes were still on us as I collected my board and towel and walked back up the stairs to my truck.

To this day, years later, Dee still tries to follow me surfing. I keep her in my truck with the windows part-way down. As I walk towards the beach she hangs out the window howling loudly at this injustice. I just chuckle ... she'll never learn.

### Sunde White

**PROFILE**

Sunde White owns a plant and garden maintenance business and is also a part time illustrator. She currently lives and surfs in San Francisco with her little brown dog, Dee.

*Surfers Preparing for Really Big Waves. From "Riding Giants." Photo Courtesy of Sony Picture Classics*

*As a lifelong surfer I never feel as much Aloha as when I am
in the water. There is no place of prayer that compares to the
ocean. Perhaps the most exhilarating thing about surfing is that it
addresses all of man's struggles: Man vs. Man, Man vs. Nature,
and Man vs. Self. It is always a challenge, yet it is always a
place of inner peace.*

*When I graduated from college I took a solo surf trek through
Costa Rica. One of the most vivid memories was how every
morning at Playa Tamarindo I was beaten into the water by
a group of very zealous surfers: three local dogs. Without fail,
every morning before sunrise they would be in the water playing,
wrestling, and surfing. A memory like that makes me wonder
"what better place to be with man's best friend than at man's
favorite playground."*

**Matt Meyerson**
**The Groundswell Society**

The Groundswell Society is a philanthropic and
educational California non-profit organization dedicated
to the global surfriding community.

# Radical Moves the Surf Dog Can't Make

Images this page and opposite page top,
courtesy of Surfing Australia

*Brad Gerlach tows Mike Parsons into the ride of his life at Jaws. From the film, "Billabong Odyssey" © 2003 Arenaplex*

# Radical Moves the Surf Dog Can Make

*Buddy shows moves that only a dog with a towline can master*

Photographs courtesy of Bruce Hooker

Photograph courtesy of the Landrum Family

# Tails from the Nose: Toby the Thrasher Dog

Toby, the Landrum's Westie, adds great personality to the family. Often viciously attacking bugs in the house or squirrels in the yard, he is not one to be messed with.

His extremely social personality allows him to place himself squarely in the middle of any conversation or game.  His easy-going side accommodates the Landrum kids in activities like skateboarding and obstacle courses (with enough snack incentive).

Toby plays hard, works hard, sleeps hard, has a great appetite, and is completely entertaining in all his Thrasher Westie ways.

PROFILE

# Howlin' Gear
## for the Surf Dog & Crew

Ask any Surf Dog and they will tell you, "Make sure there's meat on that bone," which to a dog means, "The right tool for the right job!" At the beach, this recommendation refers not only to boards and lifejackets, but also to swimsuits and other accessories for the human component of the crew. However, before you just give the pup any old board and let them cruise into the swells, the following are a few good choices to consider:

### Longboards

A longboard is generally longer and broader than other boards (bodyboards, shortboards); often over nine feet long. Longboards have better balance for most dogs. They tend to go straighter, and therefore don't veer too far off course or cut unintentionally. A lot of dog riders begin on the longboard also because there is space on the back for a human partner to sit, paddle, steer, hold onto the dog, or ride tandem. Plus, if the dog walks around a little there's enough room that it won't fall off the board immediately. If the dog is bigger than a labrador, then a longboard is pretty much required.

*Opposite Page: "Chopper" the
VonZipper Surf Dog*

Photograph courtesy of Von Zipper and Billabong

## Shortboards

Shortboards are usually 5-7 feet in length, and are used for greater maneuverability and speed. For good surfers a shortboard is what a lot of people like to ride to practice moves, cuts, etc. The smaller size and other features make it much more maneuverable than the longboard. For dogs, this maneuverability can be a little tricky, especially if the dog is big. Not a lot of room to stand on, and when the dog shifts weight interesting things may happen. Also, if the waves are choppy you might see a lot more wipeouts. But that's not to say that you shouldn't try it. Dogs can surf on the shortboard, just not as easily at first. If that's the board you have, then that's the board you should use. Just like with beginner surfers, have them try it close to the shore before they go farther out.

## Boogie Boards, Body Boards & Skim Boards

Bodyboards are small-sized foam boards ridden lying face down or on one's knees, often with swim fins. Smaller than a shortboard, these can be used to start learning how to surf right on

*Right: A Gordon and Smith Body Board*

the beach, where the waves meet the sand. They are also a good size for relatively small dogs, as well as child companions.

## Soft-top Boards

Those poor doggy toes and toenails just aren't the best for getting a grip on smooth, wet surfaces. They're nowhere near as effective as your semi-prehensile primate toes. Without some sort of friction, a dog staying on a surfboard is doing a better balancing act than an Olympic gymnast.

Give the pup a leg up with soft-top board.

*Above & Right: The Liquid Shredder ® "soft" surfboard brings the thrill of surfing to kids and the beginners*

## Surf Wax

Also known as 'doggy chew toys.' Keep safely stashed away.

## Lifejackets

A few questions to ask before you think about lifejackets and whether your dog might want one:

•Who is taller?

•Who can hold their breath underwater?

•Who can grab onto the board if they get tired?

•Who has semi-webbed toes?

•Who can call for help?

•Who brought the dog out to surf?

Still think that you're the only one who might need a lifejacket?

*"I may be cute, but I'm not stupid!*
*Where is my life jacket?"*

Left: Full-body Men's
Wetsuit (Billabong)

Right: Wetsuit for Women
(Roxy's "Cell")

Left: Long-sleeve Rash
Guard (Billabong)

## Wetsuits

Teaching a dog to surf can take some time, which means that you're going to be in the water for quite awhile. Usually being in cooler water isn't a problem since you're keeping busy paddling, surfing, etc., but since your dog isn't going to always meet your level of activity, you might want to make sure that you're staying warm and enjoying the experience.

Remember, if you're not enjoying it, neither is the dog.

## Beach wear

Because we all want to look good, and with a surfing dog and the right outfit we all look even better.

*Left: There are all types of acceptable and stylish beachwear*

*photograph courtesy of Roxy*

## Surf Dog Advertisements

Chopper is the surf dog of one of the VonZipper athlete's roommates. The owner's name is Kerry "Dunny" McDonough, and Chopper's 'Uncle' is professional skateboarder Al Partenan. Photographer EG Fratantaro works for skateboard shoe company, Globe.

Though this cool canine does not surf, Chopper became a surf dog celebrity when featured in VonZipper ads that ran in many international Surf and Skate magazines. Chopper also was a cornerstone for VonZipper's point-of-purchase marketing within retail stores.

Because of her chill surf dog attitude, VonZipper received many emails and phone calls inquiring about purchasing Chopper and her posters. VonZipper does not sell either of these items.

As with many sports, surfing's general popularity is partially driven by superstar athletes, coolness, danger, and a dash of sex appeal. This can be seen in the types of ads commonly printed for surf and water sports products. In the past, men were the target audience, but over time women have emerged as a significant force in surfing. Though many ads photograph women as a source of visual appeal, others use women as the actual heroes of the publication. Child surfers, or groms, are also increasingly being utilized as figures of inspiration for the surf crowd.

The question we ask sponsors is, "Will dogs finally have their day in the sun?"

*As I get older, I have been thinking about getting a Guide Dog to bark when a set wave is coming.*

**Michael W. Spence**
**Coalition of Surfing Clubs**
**Long Beach District, California**

This page: Examples of the changing face of surf advertising, from print to DVDs. Women and children have gained more visibility.

# Tails from the Nose:
# Part-Ex and John-Paul

**P**art-Ex is one of the most fearless daredevil dogs in the world. Not only does he surf, but he also wind surfs, cliff dives, and kayaks. Of course, he doesn't do this alone. His human companion, John-Paul Eatock, is also his partner in extreme sports. They have scaled so many of these athletic heights together that Part-Ex, which is said to sometimes stand for "Part-Dog, Part-Extreme," has been featured in a number of newspapers, magazines, and television broadcasts. This includes the show, "Dogs with Jobs," though it is

*Part-Ex: "Part-Dog, Part-Extreme Known as the World's Mos Extreme Sports Dog by the Guinness Book of Record*

National Geographic Channel, Courtesy of Cineflix

PROFILE

difficult to say if Part-Ex considers this profession a job.

Ironically, Part-Ex did not start off as a danger dog. He initially wanted to be a nice house dog, but his Jack Russell terrier energy level made that an unlikely scenario. His first owner introduced Part-Ex to the beach, spending time walking and exploring the shore. When that owner was away on vacation, he stayed with his part-time dogsitter, John-Paul.  Part-time eventually became full-time, and the surf dog world has never been the same.

John-Paul first discovered Part-Ex's taste for extreme sports when he found that the dog liked to jump into waterfalls. Not once, but over and over again. After that experience, John-Paul included Part-Ex in all of his own outdoor activities. Or it could be said that Part-Ex came along just to make sure that John-Paul was safe and not doing anything too foolish... at least not without him!

Wearing his lifejacket, Part-Ex has traveled the United Kingdom and beyond, snapping up new challenges. His competitive spirit has garnered him many titles, but his most prestigious is from the Guinness Book of Records, which calls him the canine performer of the most extreme sports.

National Geographic Channel, Courtesy of Cineflix

# Tips for the Surf Dog

**A Bonfire Chat with
Surf Dog Companions John-Paul Eatock,
Bruce Hooker, and Ed Hepp**

**QUESTION**:  How did you first teach your surf dog to surf

J-P: I didn't teach him to surf- he picked it up himself. I was dragging the board out behind me one day, and turned around to find him on it and ready to go- since then there has been no turning back for the little hound!

**QUESTION**:  Have you ever attempted to teach other dogs to surf? What size board does your surf dog use?

J-P: Never tried it with other dogs.  I have not seen any other dogs that naturally want to get out of the car to go and woof at waves for hours on end, or woof at fast moving river water whilst jumping in over and over again.  This is what Part-Ex does naturally with no prompting at all!

BRUCE: I have not attempted to teach other dogs to surf. Our Aussie shepherd loves the water, but doesn't want to surf. That is actually an interesting question.

**QUESTION**:  Did you ever use food as a reward?

J-P: Never as he loves to be in, woof at and run towards any form of moving water- food would only be a distraction!

BRUCE: We never used food as a reward. Buddy just has been surf stoked from the first time he surfed.

ED: Never.

**QUESTION**:   Do you think that some dog's have an aptitude for surfing, or that any dog can do it?

J-P: I can only say that as far as Part-Ex is concerned, it is all natural. I have no doubt however that with patience a dog that is happy in water can be trained to surf.

BRUCE: I don't think very many dogs can actually surf. My feeling is that they must first be very comfortable in the water, just like a human, learning to surf. Jack Russell Terriers have a personality that is very obsessive when they get on a task, be it Frisbee, ball, digging a hole, etc. Buddy just became obsessed with his surfing, and really enjoys it. He sees everyone at the beach surfing and playing, and he wants to participate and be part of it.

**QUESTION**: What's the deepest water you think it's safe for a dog to surf in (knowing they may wipe out)

J-P: It's not the deepest water that is the problem (Part-Ex is sponsored by a watersports clothing company called Nookie so has a buoyancy aid etc and depth is not the issue), rather it is the shape and size of the wave. If it is too steep, it may take Part-Ex down for a little too long, so we tend to stick to more spilling waves that are about 3 feet in warmish water (he has little body fat so gets cold quickly)

BRUCE: The depth of the water is not the issue. Actually, you want the water to be deep enough that you don't hit bottom when you wipe out. The key safety issue is how far from shore you are, and if the dog swims well enough to reach shore not if, but when, you wipe out. I was a pool lifeguard for several years during college, and there are several other issues such as the slope of the ocean bottom, steep or gentle, currents, rolling or steep waves.

**QUESTION**: How long did it take for your surf dog to learn to the best way to stay on the board? (1 try, 10 tries, 30 tries, etc.)

J-P: He is a first timer and did it straight away.  I think his low centre of gravity, short legs and his tip top fitness helps.

BRUCE: Buddy learned within maybe 20 tries that he had to adjust his weight and center of gravity while riding waves, from several wipeouts. He tended to pearl, or catch a rail and the board with tip over, with him going in the drink. It was probably his 3rd session that he really started to adjust.


**QUESTION**:  Was there anything you could do to help him learn these surfing techniques?

J-P: Non- except for putting a pad on the board or craft to help him grip better.

BRUCE: During takeoffs, he used to be facing me and the wave, riding in backwards. It looked somewhat awkward. Buddy learned to turn around during takeoffs as I let go of the board. I now tell him, turn around, and he usually does to insure success.


**QUESTION**:  When your dog wipes out, does that mean he fell off, or did the wave actually crest on him?

J-P: Part-Ex gets wiped out both ways, however he usually manages to stay on all the way to the beach and then jumps off where it is deep enough for him to walk.

BRUCE: Wipe outs vary; sometimes he catches a rail or pearls, other times, the wave will close out and possibly knock him off. He has learned to stay low when the wave is critical for success.

**QUESTION**: How does your dog get back on the board after a wipe out?

J-P: I usually grab him by the handle on his buoyancy aid and put him back on.

BRUCE: Buddy gets back on his board in different ways. If he rides a wave all the way into shore, the surge will actually start to take the board back out to sea, Buddy will actually put his front paws on the board, and push it back out to deeper water, then jumping on it with all four legs, just balancing, waiting for me to take him back out, or ride the shorebreak in by himself. I usually bodysurf the next wave in after Buddy rides in to get him. Buddy greets me at the shore barking, telling me to get his board, so we can get another wave. I can give Buddy the command, "go get your board", and he will run to wherever the board is, and jump on it. He has learned to skimboard in the past few months. I take his board, throw it for him in shallow water out towards the surf, he runs and jumps on the board, and rides it out. He has become very good at it, except when I time it to where he may run into a big shorebreak wave that hammers him. He has learned to get out of the wave. He can anticipate a wipeout, and gets out of the way. When I take him out in between waves he stands on the board, and does a balancing act. He adjusts to go over the waves. Sometimes I have to push his board up over a breaking wave and he will lung off the board over the wave to make it, and not get hammered. He wears a lifejacket from "Ruffwear", with a web handle, that I can grab him like a briefcase and put back on the board, if he can't swim, and get himself back up.

ED: When he wiped out or the wave ended he'd just swim in to shore and then run back out to meet me coming in to get the board. I'd encourage him to come back out for more and if he wanted to he did. After doing this a few times, he got tired and decided to stay on the beach and make friends with some local fishermen who'd been watching. I think he rode 4 waves.

**QUESTION**:  Do you ever paddle out with the dog on the board, or does he always swim out?

J-P: I usually paddle with him on the board as he is so small.  Sometimes when I am in the line up he has shown up after seeing me from a nearby headland and comes on over for a quick dip.

BRUCE: Buddy paddles out with me most of the time on the nose. He loves it, and I enjoy having him. I only take him out at gentle breaks that I know I will be successful. We rode a 4-5 foot wave one day because we had to. We got caught inside on a set, and we had to turn around and go, or get slammed -- but we made it. Buddy took the opportunity to jump off the board when we got near shore, which is his way of telling me he is done. Our local spot "school house" is close to shore, and if I go for a surf and leave Buddy on the beach while I am surfing, more times than not, he will swim out to join me.

ED: Mugs swims out and the waves are small enough that I'm standing on the bottom. I'd like to get a big enough board to paddle him out on the nose and ride tandem, but I haven't tried that yet.

**QUESTION**: Are there any brands of boogie boards or soft top boards that you recommend?

J-P: No

BRUCE: We have used the original Moorey Boogie board for Buddy. The board need to have some rocker, it is more forgiving, if it is too stiff and flat, it catches rails to easily. We have surfed on Moorey Doyle surfboards, and SurfTech soft tops. His claws will tear up a soft board after a period of time, not to mention that he likes to chew on his board after it gets to shore. The soft tops will last longer for tandem surfing. You have to realize that the board can hurt the dog if you wipe out, so I prefer a softer board while tandem surfing with Buddy or my son Matthew. Yes, all 3 of us have ridden a wave or two on the same board.

**QUESTION**:  Do you see leashes as functional for safety in surfing?

J-P: Yes- so that boards don't hit other water users, but not a necessity.

BRUCE: Leashes are a safety item for surfing most spots. It saves your board from getting far away from you as well as hitting someone else if you lose it. Particularly with all the new longboarders joining surfing. It can also save your board from the rocks. There are some places and waves that a leash is not appropriate. I surf with a leash.

ED: I don't think a dog should be on a leash in the water. Dogs are strong swimmers and are better off left to swim freely. A leash could hamper the dog's ability to move the way it needs to and be more of a safety problem than an aide.

**QUESTION**: Are there any safety items that you've noticed would help dogs who surf?

J-P: Yes, his buoyancy aid!

BRUCE: Some people are starting to wear helmets in surfing. Surfing is getting more popular, and many beginners don't know the rules or etiquette of surfing. Some really critical waves warrant wearing a helmet Booties are essential in many rocky bottom breaks. Ear plugs can save your ears from swimmers ear after a prolonged surfing career in cold windy waters.

**QUESTION**: What kind of lifejacket does the dog use (brand, size, etc.).

J-P: Part-Ex is sponsored by Nookie (www.nookie.co.uk), he has one that is made to fit, out of neoprene and foam.

BRUCE: Buddy wears a Ruffwear brand life vest. He is a size small. Ruffwear has a website. It was designed for dogs that take raft trips.

**QUESTION**: When the dog is tired of wiping out, what does he do? Does he show hesitancy to continue, or to do it again later?

J-P: He usually swims either to the board for another go, or towards the shore if he has had enough.

BRUCE: Yes, when he is tired, or finished, he shows hesitancy. He usually runs into warm dry sand and tries to roll in it to get warm. The water where we surf is usually between 60-68 degrees, and he does get cold after about an hour, except on hot summer days. He will take a break, and want to go again later. Sometimes he will search the beach for someone else to take him. We have to get him to leave some people alone at times, he will try and ride their board if it washes into shore unoccupied.

**QUESTION**: In your opinion, how long do you really think it takes to teach a dog to surf (amateur level of course). Is that when working with them once a week, twice a week, every day?

J-P: Straight away in Part-Ex's case- no teaching required at all

BRUCE: Hard to say. I would have to take another dog and work with them. We are a beach culture family, and have always walked the dogs on the beach. Buddy has always been around the water. If a dog wasn't comfortable around water, it could take forever. I have seen Labrador retrievers jump on Buddy's board. I would want to work with them 2 or 3 times, if they are comfortable in the water. Other dogs seem jealous when they see Buddy ride his board into shore. Buddy got into a fight once when another dog tried to jump on his board, he is very possessive!

ED: That's kind of a funny question. Amateur level? Is there anything else?

**QUESTION**: Have you seen other surfing dogs before? How would you describe many of the owners (include sex, age, personality, etc.)?

J-P: Yes, Max from West Wales Windsurfing owned by Pete Bounds in Wales. Pete is a watersports enthusiast and his dog stands on the board for giggles!

**QUESTION**: Why do you think people want their dogs to surf?

J-P: It is not me that wants him to surf, it is him that wants him to surf- honestly!

**QUESTION**: What was the "coolest" thing you have ever seen a dog do at the beach or on the water?

J-P: Part-Ex is happy cliff jumping into water by himself from about 14 feet- now that is cool for a small dog. He goes head first - check out the website www.x-woof.com and go to cliff jump.

**QUESTION**: Based on your experience and your observations, what would you conclude are the best ways that people went about helping, training, or encouraging their dogs to surf?

J-P: Only do it if the dog is interested in water and enjoys swimming, otherwise teach them something else. I have just been lucky with Part-Ex that he suits my lifestyle with no training at all- I only wish that I owned him when he had testicles as he would make the perfect offspring for surfers around the world!

**QUESTION**: Can you list all of the media in which you and your surf dog have appeared?

J-P: The list is very long...

- The Daily Mail
- The Times
- The Guardian
- The News of the World
- National Geographic- Dogs with Jobs
- Blue Peter
- The Big Breakfast
- Opened the Ski and Snowboard Exhibition at Alexandra Palace (He snowboards too!)
- The BBC News- several times
- Local news and press
- Sky TV News

- Press around the world- even a newspaper I came across whilst in Zimbabwe!

**BRUCE: Here's a few:**

- Ventura County Star
- Amazinganimalactors.com
- Japanese TV documentary- Global Photo Associates
- Pet Star  - Animal Planet Television
- Los Angeles Times
- MSNBC
- Lido Yatch Expo

**ED:** A book about golden retrievers by photographer Denver Bryan, called "Golden Rules."

*This page and next: Surf Dog culture has made it big in retail clothing stores and surf shops, and has fans of all ages.*

# Great Surf Dog Beaches

*For surf dogs and dog lovers I recommend "It's Beach," a great dog beach in Santa Cruz. Dogs are allowed before 10:00 AM and after 4 or 5 PM. It is located immediately "North" of the lighthouse in Santa Cruz on West Cliff Drive.*

**Bob Strickland,
Santa Cruz Surf Museum**

Finding a good, safe, and legal beach for dog surfing can be a challenge, especially with constant changes to local leash laws, the environment, and the use of performance-enhancing dog food. But dog surfing experts say that the following locales are good bets. This list does not take into account the scores of beaches where you can take a dog for a stroll on the sand, irrespective of surfing ability.

Dog Beach - San Diego, California
Stinson Beach, California
Muir Beach, California
Rincon Point, (backside), California
Padero Lane, Carpinteria, California
Inside Point, Ventura, California
School House, Ventura, California
Little Sunset, Oxnard, California
Doheney State Beach, Dana Point, California
Tairua, Coromandel Peninsula, New Zealand
Whitesands, Wales, UK
Freshwater West, Wales, UK
Newgale, Wales, UK
Gwithian, Cornwall, UK
Praa Sands, Cornwall, UK
Fistral, Cornwall, UK
Town Beach, Cornwall, UK

# Surf Dog Lingo

**Aloha**
Hawaiian expression for Hello, Good-bye, or Good Fortune.

**Backside**
Surfing with your back facing the wave

**Bodyboard**
Bodyboards are small-sized usually foam boards ridden lying face down or on one's knees, often with swim fins.

**Bodysurf**
Surfing without a board while lying face down.

**Crest**
The top of the wave.

**Double Overhead**
Waves twice as tall as the surfer.

**Drop-in**
1) Refers to surfing the face of the wave right after catching it. 2) Getting on a wave already ridden by another surfer. Not cool.

**Grom, Grommet, Grommit**
Young surfer, about 16 years old or less.

**Hang Ten**
A longboard trick where the surfer places both feet so that all ten toes hang over the front edge of the surfboard.

**Leash**
1) A cord attached to the surfer's ankle and the board that prevents the board from drifting away from a surfer in the water. 2) A cord used to keep a dog close to its owner. Never used on surfboards.

**Line-up**
The area in water where surfers wait for approaching waves.

**Longboard**
A longboard is generally longer and broader than other boards (bodyboards, shortboards); often over nine feet long.

**Pearl**
A wipeout or falling off of the front of the board caused when the front tip, or nose, of the board digs down into the water.

**Rail**
The edge of the surfboard that separates the top from the bottom.

**Set**
A series or group of waves.

**Shortboard**
Shortboards are usually 5-7 feet in length, and are used for greater maneuverability and speed.

**Take off**
To catch the wave and ride.

**Wipeout**
To end the surf ride, either by falling off or being knocked off.

# Resources

Cineflix Productions Inc.
Producer of Dogs With Jobs TV Series
5505 St Laurent Blvd. Suite 3008
Montreal, Quebec, H2T 1S6
Tel: 514 278-3140
Fax: 514 279-3165
info@cineflix.com

The Surfrider Foundation
National Office
San Clemente, CA
(local chapters throughout USA and International)
www.surfrider.org

Canine Partners For Independence
www.c-p-i.org.uk

Dawn Animal Agency
www.dawnanimalagency.com

Guiding Eyes for The Blind
www.guiding-eyes.org

Hearing Dogs for Deaf People
www.hearing-dogs.co.uk

Paws With A Cause
www.pawswithacause.org

Celebrity Dogs
www.celebritydogs.com

Guide Dogs For the Blind
www.guidedogs.com

Guiding Eyes for The Blind
www.guiding-eyes.org

American Kennel Club
www.akc.org

American Rare Breeds Association
www.arba.org

Canadian Kennel Club
www.ckc.ca

SurfPulse, surf reports, news, and features for surfers from Northern California and the rest of the world.
www.surfpulse.com

SURF STYLE, exhibits, art, books and events on Surf Culture
www.surfstyle.org

Surfing Australia, the OFFICIAL information site for the sport of surfing in Australia. which draws information from its vast network of state branches, national circuits, clubs and affiliated organisations.
www.surfingaustralia.com

Surfn' Santa Cruz
rls@cruzio.com

Surfline.com
The most comprehensive surf-related web site on the Internet. Surf cams, reports, features, travel...
www.surfline.com

Surf Diva
World's 1st Surf School for Women & Girls*!
(with "Guys on the Side!")
www.surfdiva.com

Endless Summer Surf Camp
PO Box 414, San Clemente, CA 92674
Tel: 949498-7862
www.endlesssumersurfcamp.com

Oceanside Surf Sessions
2955 Butler St. Oceanside, CA 92054
Tel: 760 757-2601
lags@cox.net.com
www.surfinstitute.com

Santa Cruz Surf School
PO Box 3600, Santa Cruz, CA 95063
Tel: 831 426-7072
www.santacruzsurfschool.com

Surf Sessions
PO Box 11, Del Mar, CA 92014
Tel: 858 481-1450
www.surfsessions.com

Surf Diva Surf School
2160 Avenida de la Playa, La Jolla, CA 92037
Tel: 858 454-8273
Fax: 858 454-8505
isashine@yahoo.com
www.surfdiva.com

Corky Carroll's Surf School
624 20th Street, Huntington Beach, CA 92648
Tel: 714 969-3959
Fax: 801 740-4587
surfschool@hotmail.com
 www.surfschool.net

Surf Class Surf School
519 San Clemente St. Ventura, Ca. 93001
Tel: 805 648-2662
info@surfclass.com
www.surfclass.com

Davey Smith's Surf Academy
222 Meigs Road #20, Santa Barbara, California
93109
Tel: 805 965-7341
surfing@surfinstruction.com
www.surfinstruction.com

The Richard Schmidt School of Surfing
314 Dofour St., Santa Cruz, CA 94060
Tel: 408-423-0928
Fax: 408-423-0928
www.richardschmidt.com

Club Ed Surf School
2350 Paul Minnie Avenue, Santa Cruz, CA 95062
Tel: 831 464-0177 or 1-800-287-SURF
Fax: 831 464-0107
clubed@sbcglobal.net
www.club-ed.com

Surf Camp Pacifica
P.O. Box 1244, Pacifica, CA 94044
Tel: 650 738-5757
soulsfr@aol.com
www.surfpacifica.com

Surf Sisters
1180 Pacific Rim Hwy, Tofino, BC Canada
Tel: 877 724-7873 or 250 725-4456
info@surfsister.com
www.surfsister.com

NexGeneration Surf School
218-A E. Eau Gallie Blvd.
PMB 135, Indian Harbor Beach, FL 32937
Tel: 321 591-9577
bgflail@aol.com
www.nexgensurf.com

North Shore Surf Camps
Hawaii
www.northshoresurfcamps.com

Coalition of Surfing Clubs
www.surfclubs.org

California Surf Museum
223 North Coast Highway
Oceanside, CA 92054
Tel: 760 721-6876
www.surfmuseum.org

Surf History.com/
www.surfhistory.com/

Wet Sand, the ultimate surfing destination on
the internet.
www.wetsand.com

Surf Art
www.surfart.com

Boardfolio.com
www.boardfolio.com

Billabong
www.billabong.com

Body Glove
www.bodyglove.com

Roxy
www.roxy.com

Ripcurl
www.ripcurl.com

Reef
www.reefbrazil.com

Von Zipper
www.vonzipper.com

Quiksilver
www.quiksilver.com

Ruffwear
www.ruffwear.com

Nookie
www.nookie.co.uk

Lost Enterprises
www.lostenterprises.com

# Index

*I think it would be cool to be able to take a dog surfing with me because I love my dog Daisy almost as much as I love my wife! My last dog Mossi surfed over at Tairua, where I live. For me the most important things to have when taking a dog to surf are a surfboard and my wife!*

**Luke Millen**
**New Zealand's Surfing Magazine**

*Big wave surfer Laird Hamilton demonstrates a longboard in "Riding Giants." Photo courtesy of Sony Picture Classics*

# Paid Announcement

In order to Present a Fair & Balanced View, the following is a Canine Editorial on this book.

### Avon the Dog's Analysis of
### Dog Body Design and Humans

**Avon**: "Ruff, ruff. Growl. Grrrrr, grrrr. Growl, growl, ruff. Grrrrr. Yip! R'uh R'oh! Growl, growl, ruff. Grrrrr. Grrrrr. Grrrrr. Ruff, ruff. Growl. Ruff, ruff. Growl. Yip! Yip! Bark, bark!"

**Human Translation:** "I love people, but they ...

- Have no fur on their bodies
- Have no claws
- Have no fangs
- Have no drool
- Have dry noses
- Have no tails
- Pick things up with their front paws
- Have ears that don't move
- Eat burnt meat and plants
- And, know only a few useful words
     ('Stop. Stay. Good. Hungry. No.')

In my opinion, they should stick to surfing."